MEMORIALS
TO THE DEAD

MEMORIALS TO THE DEAD

A Journey into England's Most Unusual Graves

KATE CHERRELL

FONTHILL

First published in Great Britain in 2026 by
Fonthill
An imprint of
Pen & Sword Books Ltd
Yorkshire – Philadelphia
www.fonthill.media

ISBN 978-1-03615-658-9

A CIP catalogue record for this book
is available from the British Library.

Typeset in SabonLTStd 10/13 by
SJmagic DESIGN SERVICES, India.
Printed and bound in India by Replika Press Pvt. Ltd.

The Publisher's authorised representative in the EU for product
safety is Authorised Rep Compliance Ltd., Ground Floor,
71 Lower Baggot Street, Dublin D02 P593, Ireland.
www.arccompliance.com

For a complete list of Pen & Sword titles please contact
PEN & SWORD BOOKS LIMITED
George House, Units 12 & 13, Beevor Street, Off Pontefract Road,
Barnsley, South Yorkshire, S71 1HN, England
E-mail: enquiries@pen-and-sword.co.uk
Website: www.pen-and-sword.co.uk

or

PEN AND SWORD BOOKS
1950 Lawrence Rd, Havertown, PA 19083, USA
E-mail: uspen-and-sword@casematepublishers.com
Website: www.penandswordbooks.com

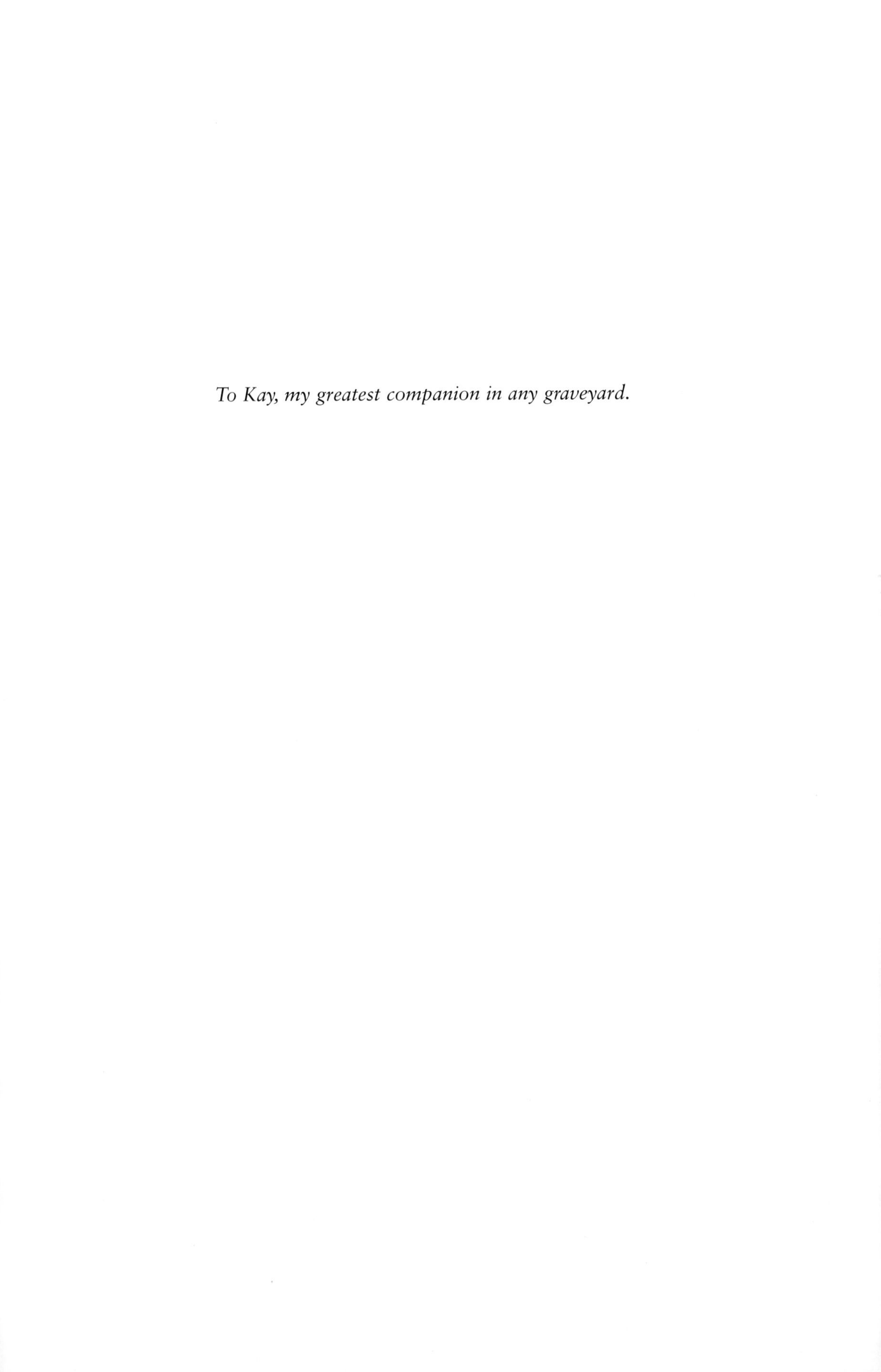

To Kay, my greatest companion in any graveyard.

Acknowledgements

I would like to extend my warmest thanks and gratitude to the following people who supported me in this project. Whether they suggested sites, offered insight, hiked to pyramids, accompanied me on ridiculous excursions to visit dead entertainers or risked heat stroke to visit the grave of a cat, thank you.

Warmest thanks to Kay Smith, without whose support this book would simply not exist. Thanks to Jay Slater who approached me about such a fulfilling niche project and all readers of BurialsAndBeyond.com. Thanks to Paul Smith, who allowed me to disrupt countless holidays and day trips with my grave obsession, Ian Boldsworth, whose tolerance in the face of regional churchyards is never bettered, my dream team of Karin 'Aunt Maud' Beasant and the lovely sweary Lisa Holman, Weird Britain's monster-hunters Andy McGrath and Matt Everett, who have been so generous with their time and resources, 'Haunted' Charlie Hall who risked sunstroke to visit mausoleums, John Newton and his knowledge of hidden gems and greyhounds, Ed and Sophie Shire for their huge hearts and grave trips, Janine Marriott and Team 46 for their unwavering support, Brian, the Uber driver from Leeds who suggested the best deathly detours, Helen Blakey, who continues to be my hero, Vaffy and Ginny for a continued source of madness and company, St-Martin-in-the-Field, Lynn Amery for her kind support, and the eternal Sidney Cherrell.

Contents

Introduction

I spent much of my childhood around graves. For many of my younger years, I would walk with my granddad twice weekly around Cleethorpes Cemetery, visiting the graves of family members who passed some forty years before I was born. My great grandparents slept in a wonky grave, slowly upended by tree roots, under a blanket of small green, glass chips. My great uncle was in a neat little grave of white granite, joined by the wife that held his last breaths in her own, leaving us shortly thereafter.

Another uncle slept overseas, a casualty of the war, his name being the only part of him that returned home intact. It too was carved into stone; a footnote on his parents' grave, slowly obscured by tufts of weeds and the rogue plastic petals of a nearby wreath. Margaret, my great-grandmother, remained a constant family presence through her grave. She was proudly Welsh, raised fourteen children in harsh circumstances, rented rooms to trippers in the summer and was always heard whistling, a beautiful, tuneful whistle that passed her descendants by. Yet none of this was on her stone, but rather just a name and a date. I could not help but wonder what the headstone would look like with a little creative license.

Wrestling with mortality is never a topic easily processed when you are still navigating the world of playground politics, but something in these excursions lit a fire in me. Instead of conventional teenage hobbies, I found solace in graveyards, searching out unusual epitaphs or secret meaning in carved flowers. Family holidays had long incorporated an excursion to some grand cemetery, where I filled up disposable camera exposures with great mournful, marble tributes to strangers I had never met and whose language I had never spoken. These graves were not simply a morbid predilection, but rather an appreciation of art, culture and story-telling, a way to connect with the legacies of others in quiet, still appreciation.

When my grandfather died, there was no great monument to his life or character. The small, black granite headstone stated his role in the family, but little else. It could not convey his love of jam sandwiches, fresh air, or strange books; those facts are doomed to die with his descendants. However, it was still, in some way, him.

Later, I briefly worked in a grand Victorian cemetery and would spend evenings wandering across the paths with a torch, imagining my own headstone—if, of course, money was no object. Exposed to graves and funerals in such high numbers, the shape of a grave, or whether a fixed grave existed at all, hardly seemed important. What is left of us, what really matters, can be told by our family and community, not carved in stone.

Yet as my love of cemeteries spread through the years, I saw instances of people who dared to buck the norm, those with the wealth, inclination or sheer creativity to memorialise their loved ones in a way they saw most befitting. Many gravestones today are designed to the allowances of council guidelines, and once-tall monuments are laid flat to protect the living. While those unusual graves left standing cannot fully represent the entire populous, they demonstrate a great diversity of lived experiences and legacies. Ultimately, cemeteries and grave sites are phenomenal sources of social history. Graves represent us all, whether we like it or not. The good, the bad and the shameful.

If an Englishman's home is his castle, then his grave is certainly his hearth. While our homes bring sanctuary, for many of us, our graves are our material legacy. They provide places to mourn and remember, but also admire, learn and acknowledge histories that would otherwise be forgotten or hidden.

This book does not seek to offer an exhaustive survey of unusual graves. To do so would take countless volumes and a rolling series, owing to the volume of beautiful and personal graves erected across the country on a daily basis. Instead, *Memorials to the Dead* offers a glimpse into the vibrant and diverse memorials that can be found in every county, cemetery and churchyard across the country. Our graves are as fascinating, important and unique as we are, and celebrating this aspect of our social history is essential.

In compiling this work, I have sought to include a diverse array of memorials and interments, including aesthetically important memorials, graves displaying historical trends, local folklore, legends, minorities, leaders, animals and those buried without names, whose exact graves were never marked. Looking beyond the visual impact of a grave allows entire histories and lives to unfold before us, demonstrating a unique and exciting thread to historical research that many other fields can never offer.

The cadaver tomb of Charles Ellis Hessey (d. 1874) is arguably the most unusual grave in York Cemetery. It depicts a recumbent figure draped in a shroud, from which a hollow face stares out eerily.

Ethel Furley (d. 1934) has one of the most endearing memorials in Yardley Cemetery, Birmingham. A likeness of Ethel sits on a bench, welcoming passers-by to join her and rest a while.

Thomas Thetcher (d. 1764), whose grave can be found in the grounds of Winchester Cathedral, died of a violent fever, contracted after drinking 'small beer' (a low-alcohol ale). Thetcher's grave became an unwitting symbol of the dangers of alcohol and went on to inspire Bill W., the founder of Alcoholics Anonymous. It is not uncommon to see sobriety tokens left on Thetcher's grave today.

In this image can be seen the entirety of this beautiful cadaver grave, including the full shape of the reclining figure. Now lost to time and covered in moss, the monument also depicts two groups of angels to either side of the deceased.

Richard Chicken (d. 1866) was a renowned local eccentric in York, and was the model for Wilkins Micawber, the optimistic yet debt-ridden character from Dickens's *David Copperfield* (1850).

This unusual memorial to Sidney John Hardwick (d. 1938) sits in Yardley Cemetery, Birmingham. It depicts the deceased sat comfortably in an armchair, offering a very cosy and appealing view from the afterlife.

A popular curiosity in the grounds of Normanby Hall in Scunthorpe is the pet cemetery of the Sheffield family, who commissioned the mansion's construction in 1825. A popular and 'spooky' attraction to visiting school parties, this quiet area of the hall's grounds is the resting place of several beloved horses and dogs, spanning nearly 200 years. This headstone marks the grave of 'Lady Sheffield's pet mare for 16 years', who died in February 1880.

In amongst the many poignant pet graves of the Normanby Hall private cemetery, some older names seem jarring and almost comical in their incongruity; take 'Smut', Mrs Lowther's pet dog who died in 1890. While her grief cannot be mocked, such a name cannot help but raise a smile from its modern connotations.

Commemorated with the light-hearted retort 'Bowled at last', this cricket-themed grave in Blackpool's Layton Cemetery is the resting place of Lancashire County Cricketer Richard Gorton Barlow (d. 1919). Barlow was a talented sportsman, playing cricket for England and refereeing a record FA Cup final. Barlow also took part in the original Ashes.

Above: This eighteenth-century grave in the churchyard of St Peter's in Chillingham bears a striking resemblance to a certain famous cartoon rodent.

Right: This headstone in the grounds of Tattershall's Holy Trinity Collegiate Church has a central glazed emblem of a lamb and staff, or 'Agnus Dei', representing Jesus, the sacrificial lamb.

The grave of Ursula Wilkinson (d. 18??) at St Edith's in Grimoldby features an elaborate weeping-angel design, recessed into the headstone with a striking dog-tooth border.

These wooden graves at St Mary the Virgin in Turville are known as 'dead boards' and contain various inscriptions.

This unusual nineteenth-century tomb at Greetwell All Saints' is a grand and curious adaptation of a cross and a traditional table tomb—a lid or ledger supported by legs.

This 'dead board' in St Mary's Church, Northchurch is a more elaborate example of the form, with ornamental crosses and a metal plaque.

Above: The Maid in Mold is believed to have been Joane Sheappeard (d. 1644), with her strange epitaph summarising her name and death date.

Left: The grave of Elizabeth Bell (d. 1951) in Fleetwood reflects the town's nautical heritage.

Amelia Edwards (d. 1892) was an accomplished writer, artist and Egyptologist whose love of Egypt and its history is shown on her grave decoration of an obelisk and large ankh.

This grave at St Aidan's in Bamburgh boasts a stark array of *memento mori* symbols that are still clear, despite weathering from the sea air.

IN LOVING REMEMBRANCE
OF
GEORGE FORMBY
(COMEDIAN)
DIED 8TH FEBRUARY 19
AGED 45 YEARS.
"After Life's Fitful Fever -
ALSO GEORGE FORMBY O.B.E.
SON OF THE ABOVE
WHO DIED 6TH MARCH 1961,
AGED 56 YEARS.
"A Tradition Nobly Upheld."

Above: The prominence of Thomas Murphy (d. 1932) in the world of greyhound racing is reflected in his grand grave in Charlton, with two large dogs depicted as if in mourning.

Right: Tucked away in Whitby Station is a tiny memorial marked 'Morte d'Arthur'. Installed by railway workers, it marks the grave of Arthur the cat (d. 1975), who lived at the station for a decade.

Opposite: George Formby (d. 1961) was one of England's greatest entertainers, with his cheeky banjolele songs a familiar sound in many households. His memorial reflects his career of performance with theatre curtains and comedy and tragedy masks.

The Ethel Preston (d. 1911) memorial in Lawnswood Cemetery, Leeds was so popular upon its unveiling in 1913 that visitors were charged a penny each to view it.

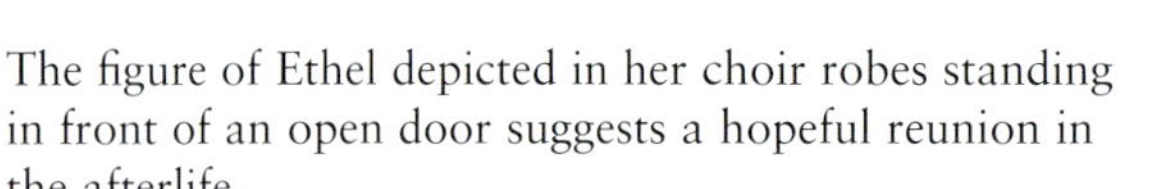

The figure of Ethel depicted in her choir robes standing in front of an open door suggests a hopeful reunion in the afterlife.

Above left: The grave of Thomas Johnson (d. 1799) in Brancepeth proudly displays the tools of his trade—barber-surgeon—including a scalpel, saw and syringe.

Above right: This well-weathered headstone in Bamburgh is the grave of carpenter Edward Johnson (d. 1746), the tools of his trade—including an axe and saw—depicted in relief.

Right: The headstone of James Emery at Northrepps (d. 184?) bears a central motif of a coffin atop a tomb, demonstrating the nineteenth-century continuation of *memento mori* symbolism.

Left: The grave of Elizebeth Ellis (d. 1722) at Northrepps features a beautiful and dense collection of *memento mori* symbolism, including skulls, hourglasses and bones.

Below: The eighteenth-century grave of Richard Smyth at Blickling is a stunning example of grave typography, topped with a skull flanked by cherubs.

Opposite: The grand grave of Hannah Adams (d. 1887) in St. Stephens, Kirkstall features an enormous cross decorated with intricate scenes from Christ's life.

Left: This seventeenth-century gravestone in Chorley is a perfect example of the rugged simplicity of earlier styles.

Below: The grand effigy tomb of Grace Darling (d. 1842) in Bamburgh is testament to her heroism and status as a local icon. Known as 'Amazing Grace', the lighthouse keeper's daughter assisted in the rescue of nine individuals from the wreck of the paddle steamer *Forfarshire* in 1838.

Tiddles was the beloved church cat of St Mary the Virgin in Fairford from 1963 until her death at the age of 17 in 1980. She attended services and regularly sat on the knees of the congregation as they worshipped.

The headstone of Henry Croft (d. 1930) has long been removed from its grave site but now stands as a memorial to London's first 'Pearly King'. Inspired by costermongers' flash outfits, he adorned his suit with buttons and raised vast amounts for charity.

Left: Emmeline Pankhurst (d. 1928) was the leader of the suffragette movement and an enduring icon in the fight for gender equality. Her memorial in Brompton is in red sandstone and features a haloed figure and angels.

Below: The tomb of John Bunyan (d. 1688) in Bunhill Fields was restored in the eighteenth century and features an enormous effigy of the man himself and bas reliefs inspired by his work 'The Pilgrim's Progress'.

Right: Malcolm McLaren (d. 2010) was a controversial music and fashion mogul and prominent figure in UK punk culture. His grave in Highgate features a prominent bronze death mask and initials.

Below: Affectionately known in Highgate as 'the horse grave', this monument marks the grave of the wife, son and stepson of John Atcheler (d. 1867). Atcheler was a slaughterhouse owner who proudly proclaimed himself 'Horse Slaughterer to Her Majesty Queen Victoria'.

The grave of artist Patrick Caulfield (d. 2005) is a spectacular example of contemporary grave architecture, designed by the artist himself.

The large grave board at Pinner dates from 1775 and is dedicated to William Kenelsby, who died at the grand age of 118.

The grave of Karl Marx (d. 1883) has been a place of protest and pilgrimage since its installation in 1956, surviving bouts of vandalism and bomb attacks. The political theorist and author of *The Communist Manifesto* was originally buried elsewhere in Highgate Cemetery, but was moved to his current plot by the Communist Party of Great Britain in 1954.

The grave of Mary Nichols (d. 1909) is often regarded as one of the most beautiful in Britain. Depicting an angel sleeping on a bed of clouds, the large vault beneath holds her remains and those of an infant grandson.

Jude Moraes (d. 1993) was a landscape gardener and broadcaster whose grave is a nod to her skilled design in summer houses.

The grave of Rebecca French (d. 1869) in Theddlethorpe is one of the country's finest examples of a felled-tree memorial. Carved from stone, the memorial is complete with breaks and sculpted fungus.

Joseph Grimaldi (d. 1837) was one of the forefathers of English pantomime and clowning. His grave references his theatrical history with decorations of theatrical masks and sits in the grounds of the renamed 'Joseph Grimaldi Park'.

Installed in Grimaldi's honour in 2010, just a few steps from his grave, are a pair of coffin 'graves' that chime when sections are depressed. Intended to be danced upon, the coffins can play 'Hot Codlins', a song popularised by Grimaldi.

Above left: This gravestone in the church of St Cyriac, Lacock is busy with death symbolism, including a broken column, heavenly rays, trumpets and flaming torches.

Above right: Dorothy Lacey's grave in Leatherhead features a large, blue barrel mosaic detail beautifully dotted with gold stars.

Douglas Adams' grave is a place of literary pilgrimage for devotees of his *Hitchhiker's Guide to the Galaxy* series, with fans leaving gifts of pens and trinkets on his plot.

1

Folklore and False and Curious Histories

Humans are an inherently visual species, recognising symbols and shapes as representative of a larger story or tradition. However, in the case of much grave decoration, these associated tales and interpretations have changed with the ebb and flow of religious, social and popular cultures. What was once a reference to mortality, piety or the transient nature of life, quickly becomes something far more exciting and, sometimes, bloodthirsty. Older graves, from the seventeenth and eighteenth centuries were often decorated with simple and recognisable *memento mori* symbolism, including skulls, winged hourglasses and crossed bones. This collection of symbols has been used as a shorthand for the inevitability of death since classical antiquity and became popular in funerary art from the seventeenth century onwards.

The Latin term *memento mori* translates to 'remember you must die' and was used profusely across church and funerary architecture as a reminder that death—and judgement—was inevitable. Prior to this, such symbols were associated with stoicism and the belief that all that passes is inevitable.

Within a Christian context, this mortal inevitability was linked to a moralistic warning and eschatological motivation to live a more virtuous life in preparation for judgement and the afterlife. Therefore, the prevalence of skulls and depictions of human remains in grave memorials was twofold: to mourn the deceased and frame them as a pious individual, and to operate as a permanent advertisement for the legitimacy of the church within whose grounds they were buried. However, from the late twentieth century, many of these graves took on lives—or afterlives—of their own. Graves bearing prominent skull motifs were frequently reframed in local folklore as being the secret resting places of pirates, owing to the skull's presence on the Jolly Roger flag.

Graves bearing skulls in coastal churchyards, as in Whitby, Southampton or any of Cornwall's many coastal burial grounds, were bound in rumours of Blackbeard and his compatriots spending eternity under a proud banner of piracy. In several towns, such as Billinge in Merseyside or Whitby on the North Yorkshire coast, graves bearing skulls and overt *memento mori* symbolism have been transformed into so-called vampire graves, where the undead rest beneath unsubtle branding. In these instances, the lure of vampiric possibility supersedes the lived reality of the decedents themselves, whose identities fade into history as gothic fiction takes a popular hold.

A curious group of graves, found within the intersection of English folklore and unusual monuments, is that of the natural rock or glacial erratic. Large stones, often believed to have been embedded in their environs during the Ice Age, were often repurposed as boundary stones or sites of ritualistic importance and attributed to druids or ancient religious orders. With their purposes or exact origins lost to time, some of these stones have been transformed by folkloric tradition to become druidic or devil's stones whereby—in the case of the stone in Bungay, Suffolk—interacting with the rock in a specific manner is connected with the casting of spells or the revelation of arcane knowledge.

In other instances, such as Woodplumpton in Preston or Great Leighs in Essex, these rocks are believed to be the grave markers for individuals accused of witchcraft, each with terrifying accompanying tales. In the case of Woodplumpton, the stone represents a non-Christian burial in a Christian churchyard, where the deceased is rumoured to be inverted vertically to prevent them from clawing through their grave and terrorising the local population. In turn, these graves have become revenants of a more superstitious time, with stories that are celebrated by those who seek to reframe the identities of persecuted and misrepresented women.

Much like burials and memorial traditions themselves, folklore and legends are ever-evolving, adapting to fit modern interests and sensibilities. In large inner-city cemeteries, many unsuspecting memorials receive modern pop-culture makeovers. In the case of Brompton in London, one nineteenth-century mausoleum has been nicknamed 'the time machine', with a history and function re-sculpted through the lens of popular culture. The mausoleum of Hannah Courtoy is a substantial structure, decorated with hieroglyphs and said to be permanently locked. Grand tales were spun regarding her life and circumstances, suggesting that her employer (or lover) had discovered the secrets of time travel, rendering the mausoleum a fully functional time machine hidden in plain sight. The visual parallels to Dr Who's TARDIS are unmistakable, thereby ensuring a mystical status that, like any touchstone of popular culture, should continue for years to come.

In the UK, most remaining burial grounds are Victorian cemeteries, designed in a conflicting age of romance, rationalism, science and superstition. Mourning united all minds. With symbolism, grave styles and materials, our ancestors were able to display their religion, wealth and status in a few simple images.

By the turn of the eighteenth century and the dawn of the Victorian era, *memento mori*-style symbolism began to fade in popularity, being replaced by a celebration of self, industrial interests and grander displays of wealth and social capital. Similarly, the manufacture of headstones and memorials changed with industrialisation and mechanical aids introduced to the field of decorative masonry. Most Victorians chose headstones and associated decoration from catalogues, with designs inspired by classical and romantic ideals. The subtle romantic symbolism of ferns, bouquets and clasped hands are inescapable across most Victorian burial spaces, signalling grief, love and reunion in a few simple motifs.

Popular trends such as the 'language of flowers' would come to influence funerary art, whereby guidebooks ascribed hidden meaning to individual blooms. Many funerary designs became homogenised across new landscapes of the dead: common Christograms such as IHS (an abbreviation of Jesus' name in Greek) and Chi Rho (an early Roman Christogram appearing as an interlocking P and X) became ubiquitous motifs for the faithful. In larger grave spaces, grander tombs followed suit. Many of the largest Victorian mausoleums are bathed in recognisable symbolism and the changing funerary trends of the romantic age. Those with the means to do so began to indulge in references to classical civilisations, ancient Egypt, and the age of the medieval Gothicism. 'Effigy tombs', with the deceased depicted in sculpture, once again became a fashionable (and simultaneously gauche) means of memorialising the wealthy dead.

The grave of Sarah Jarvis (d. 1873) in St Bartholomew's Churchyard, Corsham has become a local curiosity owing to its strange epitaph. It claims that Sarah lived to the age of 107 and grew 'fresh' (new) teeth shortly before her death.

This boulder is said to mark the grave of Margary Hilton (aka Meg Shelton) (d. 1705), a woman accused of witchcraft and known locally as the 'Fylde Hag'. Legend tells of her body being buried face-down, or vertically, with a boulder placed on top to prevent her from returning to terrorise the local community.

Known locally as 'The Vampire Grave', the coffin-shaped memorial to George and Kitty Smith (d. 1720) features beautiful examples of *memento mori* symbolism, including a skull, bat wings and ouroboros.

Above: Also known as the boundary stone between Kenilworth and Leek Wootton in Warwickshire, this stone is said to mark the grave of Betsy Smith (d. 17th century), a pauper. Local legend states that though Betsy died in Leek Wootton, her body was rolled over the parish boundary into Kenilworth to avoid footing the bill for her burial.

Right: While little is known of George and Kitty Smith's life, local legend tells of a dramatic death, invariably linked to the grave's symbolism. It was said that George worked in a nearby quarry and, while taking a break, was bitten by a snake. George lost his life to the bite and was buried in the churchyard of St Aidan's in Billinge. Kitty died shortly thereafter of a broken heart. The true cause of George's death is not known, but the legend lives on regardless.

Above: The tiny grave of Tom Thumb (d. 1620) in Tattershall is at the centre of a local legend and enduring English fairytale. Reportedly dying at the age of 101, he was said to stand 18.5in. tall and have enjoyed a wealth of wild adventures, which were chronicled in popular seventeenth-century pamphlets.

Left: While the epitaph of Mary Gibson's grave in Folkingham is hard to discern, it remains terribly ominous, leading with 'UNCEREMONIOUS DOOM. "The thunder clap was heard, the bolt was felt before it was heard, such was the will of heaven."'

In the centre of a field of cows in Hertfordshire sits the grave of England's last executed highwayman, James Blackman 'Robert' Snooks (d. 1802). After robbing a post boy in Boxmoor, he was caught and executed close to the place he committed the crime.

The sealed mausoleum of Hannah Courtoy (d. 1849) is believed by some to be a functioning time machine or magical device, constructed by an eccentric Victorian with a love of Egyptian symbology. In reality, Courtoy's tomb is a beautiful example of mid-Victorian Egypt-inspired British design.

While historical records claim that the body of William Shakespeare (d. 1616) lies within this tomb at Holy Trinity Church, Stratford, countless mysterious tales surround his remains, including stories of a curse, a missing skull and stolen identities.

The grave of George Lewis (d. 1830) in Warnford depicts how an accident while woodcutting resulted in his death. Legend says this was a punishment from God for working on Sundays.

Above: Ann Rothwell's headless effigy at Lancaster Priory has several associated legends. One version states that in an attempt to delay her husband's execution, Ann climbed the clock tower, desperately hoping to stop it striking. In her haste, she lost her balance and fell, dying instantly. She is thought to haunt the local environs as a 'white lady'.

Right: The grave of Hannah Twynnoy (d. 1703) is not unusual in style, but rather in circumstance and epitaph. Hannah was the first person to be killed by a tiger in the UK. When a travelling menagerie set up at her place of work, she reportedly entertained herself by provoking a tiger, ignorant of the danger in which she had placed herself. When the tiger broke free of its cage, Hannah was fatally wounded.

Left: Charles Thompson (d. 1784) was a successful businessman and philanthropist with a fear of having his remains disturbed. He was buried 18ft deep on a hill in Mansfield.

Below: Thompson's large enclosed grave is a continued reminder of his decades of selfless, charitable work.

Opposite: This long grave in Hathersage is known locally as 'Little John's Grave', marking the resting place of the legendary Robin Hood's right-hand man.

BURIED
LITTLE JOHN
LIEUTENANT OF
ROBIN HOOD
CARE OF THIS
UNDER TAKEN BY
ORDER OF
FRIENDLY SOCIETY

Left: While there is no evidence that Little John ever existed, this sizeable plot matches his large stature and attracts tourists and Robin Hood scholars alike.

Below: While this tomb in Essendon may look unremarkable, it is the resting place of the Rev. Richard Orme (d. 1845). Fearful of being buried alive, he insisted on building a tomb with a lockable door. He was buried with the key, alongside a loaf of bread and jug of wine in case he awoke. The door was finally sealed in 1881.

Above: The 15ft-tall pyramid at Nether Wallop is considered to be the first funerary pyramid in Britain. Inside are the remains of the eccentric death-obsessed physician Dr. Francis Douce (d. 1760), who had the structure perfectly placed along meridian lines.

Right: The tomb of Lady Anne Grimston at Tewin is the focus of ominous local legend. It is said that Anne did not believe in life after death, saying on her deathbed, 'If indeed, there is life hereafter, trees will render asunder my tomb.' Whether there is truth in the tale or not, her grave continues to move at the mercy of enormous roots.

The effigy tomb to Anne (d. 1806) and Thomas Dunn (d. 1827) has an identity problem. Despite the epitaph, it is argued that another woman, Caroline Dunn of Madeira, had the tomb commissioned for her husband Thomas, but was not buried in it herself, having it simply bear her likeness.

The confusion surrounding the interment does not distract from the striking memorial, showing a woman in repose.

Right and below: Jemima Ayley (d. 1860) is depicted as an effigy atop her tomb in Charlton Cemetery, said to be dug at a depth of 22ft and furnished with a table and chairs for visitors!

Known locally as 'the floating coffin', this strange memorial to William (d. 1809) and Agnes (d. 1841) Loudon features a sarcophagus 'floating' in the middle of a large stone wedge. Local legend says that their son would receive sums of money from his parents, as long as they were 'above ground'. This curious grave was believed to be his solution. In reality, it is simply a curious design choice.

This tiny pyramid in the churchyard of St Thomas à Becket in Box is a grave with no legible inscription. It is said that the headstone was erected for a man who wished to prevent his happy widow from dancing on his grave!

Margaret 'Molly' Leigh (d. 1746) was an isolated and disfigured woman in Burslem accused of witchcraft. Upon her death, locals claimed that she was haunting the town; her grave was exhumed, her pet bird thrown into her coffin, which then reburied in a north-south direction.

The resting place of England's most infamous Highwayman Dick Turpin (aka John Palmer) (d. 1739) is said to lie in York. After Turpin was executed for horse-theft at Tyburn, his life and exploits were wildly romanticised in the nineteenth century, reframing a potentially violent criminal as a romantic hero on horseback.

Taking a closer look at the Barnardo's Memorial, it stands as a simple and profound headstone for the hundreds of children whose families were too poor to afford one themselves. After witnessing the awful realities of poverty in the East End of London, in 1868 Dr Thomas Barnardo established a mission to educate local children and provide them with a hot meal.

This tiny grave in the churchyard of St Andrews, Irby has an ominous epitaph that continues to shock and intrigue. Reading 'Nameless, be sure your sin will find you out', this ominous wording was chosen to mark the grave of an unknown newborn infant, whose remains were found in a nearby field. The wording was not intended to condemn the child, but offer a solemn, biblical threat to the unknown parents who abandoned them.

This small cluster of family graves at Searby cum Owmby in Lincolnshire offers a heartbreaking glimpse into the nineteenth-century realities of child mortality. With frequent outbreaks of contagious diseases such as scarlet fever, many families could lose multiple children within days of each other. In England and Wales in the 1850s, up to 25% of children died before they reached the age of five.

In the same churchyard of St Nicholas in Searby cum Owmby, another family's loss can be read in graduating memorial sizes, from adult to infant. While death rates in rural communities such as this were often lower than in towns throughout the nineteenth century, access to adequate healthcare was often an issue.

Above left: The headstone of Richard Maples (d. 1861) in Folkingham displays some beautiful typography, but also the reality of losing the patriarch in a large rural family, as his widow took on the sole care and financial burden of their fourteen children.

Above right: In the churchyard of St Mary's in Tetford sits a small cluster of graves of travellers, commemorating three individuals who were all killed by lightning. Tyso Boswell and his cousin Edward Hearn were killed in 1831. Their stone has been heavily amended and features multiple spelling mistakes.

Close to the Boswell and Hearn grave is that of Robert and Edward Lameman, the latter having also been killed by lightning in the late nineteenth century.

Right: A tiny gravestone stands in the grounds of Birmingham's 'Pigeon Park', marking the resting place of Nanette Stocker (d. 1819), once known as the world's smallest woman. Austrian-born Nanette was an accomplished pianist and dancer, who died in Birmingham aged thirty-nine.

Below: Nottingham's National Justice Museum is situated in the city's old gaol and courts. Beneath the slabs of the old exercise yard are the remains of many former inmates, executed on the premises. Some of these individuals were afforded rudimentary markers such as this, featuring only basic initials.

Above: The Navvies Memorial in Otley memorialises the lives of the navigators (Navvies) who died while building the Bramhope tunnel in the nineteenth century.

Left: Ian Murray Donald (d. 1935) died aged five and is memorialised in the figure of a young boy and lamb, representing both the boy himself and the piety of youth.

Opposite: In the middle of Southampton Cemetery lie several graves relating to the ex-Argentine dictator General Rosa. The grave of his grandson Manuel (d. 1926) is decorated with a book and likeness of justice, blindfolded with a sword and scales.

IN EVER LOVING
MANUEL MAXIMO

Discovered in the woods by Hamelin in Germany in 1725, a dirty non-verbal child who walked on all fours would soon be known as 'Peter the Wild Boy' and become a sensation across Europe. The first documented 'feral child', Peter became the 'pet' of the British royal family and later lived out his life at a farm in Hertfordshire, dying in 1785.

Memorialised as the 'Negro Servant' of the Earl of Suffolk, the grave of Scipio Africanus (d. 1720) is a powerful and arresting monument to the lives exploited and lost to the slave trade.

Little is known about Scipio's life, yet his painted gravestones—depicting black cherubs and *memento mori* symbols—have become a symbol of Bristol's bloody past and the ongoing fight for race equality.

Known as the Riley Graveyard, this small enclosure in Eyam holds the graves of the members of the Hancock family who died during the plague outbreak of 1666. Elizabeth Hancock buried her husband and six children in the same cemetery.

Above: After the outbreak of the plague in Eyam, the village went into 'voluntary' (how voluntary is questioned by modern historians) quarantine to prevent further spread of the disease. Two hundred sixty villagers died in a matter of months.

Left: The altruistic act of the people of Eyam is one mired in oral tradition and legend. While their graves stand as testament to their suffering during the 1666 plague, it is now believed that local religious authorities implemented the lockdown, rather than allowing the villagers to choose their own fate.

Legend states that when plague broke out in Eyam, it was the vicar, William Mompesson, who persuaded the villagers to quarantine. His own wife, Catherine (d. 1666), died during the outbreak and is buried in a grand tomb with Latin inscriptions and bold symbolism.

Known as 'The five lambs of Holcombe', this small grave with lamb sculptures memorialises the five young children who lost their lives in 1899 after falling through the ice of a nearby pond. Also remembered is a child who drowned in 1844 and was buried in the churchyard.

Above: The tomb of Dame Mary Page (d. 1729) is one of the strangest in London. Mary suffered from dropsy, which caused a build-up of fluid around her lungs. To remove this fluid, she was 'tapd', the painful experience of which is immortalised on her grave.

Left: The grave of Judith Pearce (d. 1820) in Sutton Benger is curious—both the nature of her death and the perpetrator of her murder are recorded.

3

The Age of Cemeteries

England has historically memorialised their dead with a host of different grave-marking traditions. For centuries, communal burial spaces left no requirement for individual markers. Burial grounds or chambers were marked with stones that gave no written indication as to the identities of those interred within. Instead, their vague identities would reveal themselves to archaeologists through grave goods.

The concept of eternal, undisturbed burial is a relatively modern idea. Prior to the dawn of Victorian garden cemeteries, most graves—save those of prominent persons— were expected to be re-used indefinitely. The deceased were expected to be exhumed and reinterred elsewhere, in a communal grave. While 'perpetuity burials' were the cemetery's greatest appeal, they would also be their ruin.

These new cemetery plots shaped our understanding of burial today, with the purchaser believing they possessed the sole rights to that plot indefinitely. It could not be altered, reused, reshaped or changed in any way. This would have provided mourners with great comfort, knowing their loved ones would not suffer the humiliation of exhumation and group burial, yet it monopolised a part of the cemetery grounds forever, and a full cemetery generates no future income. Subsequently, cultural ideas of jumbled and overgrown Victorian cemeteries are shaped by this flawed business model.

While countless cultures and nationalities practise differing burial traditions, England has undeniably bought into the perpetuity model. If graves are disturbed in any capacity, the act often elicits a communal primal reaction, as if doing so is an act of violence and the dead are dishonoured as a consequence. Yet our understanding of burial and remembrance will change with time, as it always has. If it was not for the grandeur of the Victorian cemetery and the lure of perpetuity, this book would not exist. We also would not possess such a rich social and artistic history in every city, town and village.

Above: Nestled in West Hill Cemetery in Winchester, the grave of George Hayes Saint (d. 1905) offers a gentle nod to British Egyptomania at the turn of the century and the prevalence of ancient Egyptian symbols and structures—such as pyramids—in English funerary decoration.

Left: This towering memorial, or 'chhatri', to Raja Ram Mohan Roy (d. 1833) in Arnos Vale is based on a traditional Bengali funerary monument and carved from Bath stone. Revered to this day, the Rajah was an influential polymath, writer, political and religious figure, campaigning for social reform, women's rights, and the end of the practice of *sati*, whereby widows were burned on the funeral pyres of their husbands.

Rev. John Adey Pratt (d. 1867) was a non-conformist preacher and Sunday school teacher. He dedicated much of his life to the temperance movement and establishing Sunday schools that offered rudimentary education to the needy. A popular pastor and influential figure in the Dings area of Bristol, the death of 'the children's preacher' was widely and deeply mourned. His memorial obelisk shows him preaching to a group of children and pointing to the heavens.

This towering gothic memorial in Tower Hamlets Cemetery takes the form of a wayside cross and marks the grave of Joseph Westwood (d. 1883) and his family. Westwood owned the iron foundry 'Thames Ironworks' on the Isle of Dogs, producing many substantial iron and steel bridges still in use worldwide. The company's football team would go on to become West Ham United, with their 'hammers' nickname originating from their ironworking roots!

This enormous memorial to Janna Haagensen (d. 1897) and her family dominates the small cemetery at Laceby in Lincolnshire. Peter Haagensen (d. 1919) was a Norwegian shipbroker and merchant who erected the grand monument to his wife Janna, depicting her at the centre of a great tree with their four children clinging to her. The Haagensen grave monument was so unusual that it became a popular tourist attraction in its own right, inspiring the production of postcards and ceramic replicas. Tourists arrived in such great numbers by the early twentieth century that their presence alone was enough to support the Laceby Tearooms and associated merchandise businesses.

The grand memorial to the Haagensen family was carved from Carrara marble and erected on the highest peak of the cemetery's grounds. Peter Haagensen originally intended the grave to be installed in Grimsby, where he had his household, but permission was refused on account of the size.

In the golden age of Victorian and Edwardian seaside holidaying, souvenirs and trinkets were inescapable, and the Karmy family produced the majority of Blackpool's tourist wares. Anthony Bulos Karmy (d. 1916) was an importer of fancy goods from the Middle East but made his home in Blackpool, where he and his family supplied tourist shops and the Piers with novelty goods for several decades. His grave depicts a lady in repose, representing eternal sleep.

The grave of Bertha 'Rubie' Broome (d. 1931) is the grander of two 'Angel of Grief' memorials in Layton, becoming a popular, if grand, representation of all-consuming grief. The original *Angel of Grief* was designed in 1894 by American sculptor William Wetmore Story and has been replicated across the world in art and funerary monuments ever since.

In funerary architecture, a broken column traditionally symbolises a life cut short, but in the case of the grave of John Arnold Parkinson (d. 1911), this column is replaced with a broken mast. Parkinson's grave commemorates his death at the age of thirty-six while committing the heroic act of attempting to save a drowning man from the Blackpool Baths. Additional symbols of a lifebelt, anchor and lifeboat recognise Parkinson's work as part of the Blackpool Lifeboat crew.

The elaborate grave of William Broadhead (d. 1931) boasts a wealth of funerary and nautical symbolism. A former mayor of Blackpool, he owned and operated seventeen theatres in the Northwest of England, nicknamed the 'Broadhead Circuit'.

The grave of journalist Alfred Halstead (d. 1907) takes the poignant form of a library book, with his date of birth and death denoted as the times the book was lent and returned.

The Hardy Tree was a beloved sight in Old St Pancras Churchyard since the poet Thomas Hardy arranged old headstones around the tree's base in 1860. A symbol of railway encroachments in the nineteenth century, the tree fell during a storm in 2022.

This enormous sculpture of a lion sits atop the grave of John Jackson, a successful bare-knuckle boxer and promoter of the sport. The grave once featured sculptures of athletes, but these are sadly long lost.

Sir Augustus Henry Glossop Harris (d. 1896) was regarded as the father of the modern pantomime, and his grave decorations reflect his theatrical background.

The tomb of John Wimble (1851) in West Norwood is an astonishing tribute to his long maritime career, featuring bas reliefs of two ships and a grand ship hull to top. In years of captaining ships, he was often—unusually—accompanied by his wife Mary, who would go on to commission this grand tomb.

The grave of Arthur Currer Briggs (1906) in Leeds features an enormous brass plaque depicting a seed-sower being overseen by an angel. He had been a mine-owner, mayor and renowned philanthropist.

Right: The grave of medieval antiquary John Britton (d. 1857) in West Norwood features an enormous rectangular granite slab.

Below: This grave in the undergrowth of West Norwood Cemetery is a powerful depiction of faith and grief.

AND OF
ANN WILSON

Opposite and right: The grave of Sam (d. 1918) and Ann Wilson (d. 1931) is the largest and most imposing in Leeds' Lawnswood Cemetery. Carved from black marble with bronze figures, it depicts faith, hope and benevolence.

Below: This grand and somewhat ecclesiastical-tinged monument to antiquarian Thomas de la Garde Grissell (d. 1847) may appear as simple stone but is in fact largely cast iron with pink granite panels.

The grand tomb of Alexander Berens (d. 1858) in West Norwood features a band of Minton tiles marked with 'B' (for 'Berens') and the image of a bear.

The successes of General Alexander Anderson (d. 1877) in the Royal Marines are commemorated in this unusual pile of carved cannonballs in Brompton Cemetery.

The memorial of Hans Schwarze (d. 1883) in West Norwood is an elaborate elevated chest tomb made of pink and grey granite with large bronze panels.

Captain Hans Robert Sparenborg (d. 1914) was one of the first officers to die in the First World War, fighting in the Kings Own Royal Regiment (Lancaster).

Watson Fothergill (d. 1928) was the leading Nottingham architect of the nineteenth century, designing over 100 buildings in the city. His unusual grave bears a Nottingham stag motif at the base.

The unusual grave of Alderman William Sylvester and his family stands prominently in Nottingham's Rock Cemetery.

Left: The once-grand sandstone grave of William Hannay (d. 1862) has suffered badly against the elements. Hannay drowned while on holiday in Sark.

Below: This dramatically weathered tomb once held a statue of a mourner but now is a mere suggestion of its former glory, all beneath a banner of 'Resignation'.

The mausoleum of Edmund Distrim Maddick (d. 1931) is of particularly unusual design, with a dramatic sloped roof and pierced cross details. Maddick was a naval surgeon who later became a pioneer of cinema. He designed the mausoleum himself a decade before his passing.

The unique landscape and sandstone outcrops of Church (Rock) Cemetery in Nottingham resulted in the creation of unique grave plots.

Above: In the hollow of Nottingham's Rock Cemetery are lines of large ledgers inscribed with hundreds of names. These are large shared paupers' graves, with more than twenty bodies in a single plot.

Right: Valentine Prinsep (d. 1904) was an artist inspired by the Pre-Raphaelite movement. He bought what he believed to be a fourteenth century chest to adorn his grave. Yet its weather-damage suggests that Prinsep was sold a replica!

Frederick Richards Leyland (d. 1892) was a shipping line owner and art patron whose distinctive tomb was designed by the Pre-Raphaelite artist Edward Burne-Jones.

The tomb of George Wombwell (d. 1850) is topped with an enormous lion, reflecting his successful career as a travelling menagerist. At the height of his success, he had fifteen wagons and bred the first lion in captivity in Britain.

Above: This large monument to concert pianist Harry Thornton (d. 1918) takes the form of a miniature grand piano. He and his wife entertained the troops during the First World War and died shortly thereafter in the 1918 flu epidemic.

Right: Tom Sayers (d. 1865) was a famous bare-knuckle fighter and heavyweight champion of England. Upon his death, an estimated 100,000 people descended upon Camden to see his funeral. His grave features a sculpture of his beloved mastiff, Lion.

The grand memorial of Sir William Casement (d. 1844), a senior figure in Bengal's government, features a chest topped with his cloak and hat, under a canopy supported by lotus leaf decorations and four Indian bearers. The railings surrounding the plot are shaped as cannon barrels. While Casement is buried in Calcutta, his widow erected this monument.

The tomb of manufacturer William Holland is an elaborate sarcophagus, supported on winged griffins. Decorations include garlands, angels and inverted torches.

Princess Sophia (d. 1848) was the fifth daughter of King George III and Queen Charlotte and died unmarried aged seventy after a life of relative isolation. Her grave features an elaborate sarcophagus on a granite podium.

Above: Alexander Nesbitt Shaw (d. 1872) of the Bombay Civil Service was buried beneath a grand monument featuring a life-sized woman mourning over an urn.

Left: Old and new are brought together in Kensal Green as a nineteenth-century angel stands beside its modern counterpart—an angel bearing a resemblance to 'The Spirit of Ecstasy', the bonnet mascot of Rolls Royce.

Right: The mausoleum of the equestrian Andrew Ducrow (d. 1842) is an elaborate and busy mixture of Greco-Egyptian symbolism, once described by *The Builder* as 'ponderous coxcombry'.

Below: The mausoleum to the Molyneux family (1866) dominates the cemetery skyline at Kensal Green and is mainly constructed of pink granite and Carrara marble.

Above and below: This large memorial features an effigy of William Mulready (d. 1863), an Irish painter who achieved success with his depictions of rural living. His grave is surrounded by miniature carvings of his paintings and carved representations of a painter's tools.

The Robert William Sievier Memorial is a curious addition to Kensal Green. The sculptor represented his parents John (d. 1837) and Frances (d. 1840), with the grand sculpture placed within the grounds of the chapel's colonnade.

The memorial to Georgiana Clementson (d. 1876) was sculpted by her father, John Graham Lough, and is set in beautiful isolation within the colonnades of Kensal Green Cemetery.

The tomb of Mary Gibson (d. 1856) is a substantial structure consisting of twelve Corinthian columns and four large angels at each corner, which once supported a central wreath.